D1196272

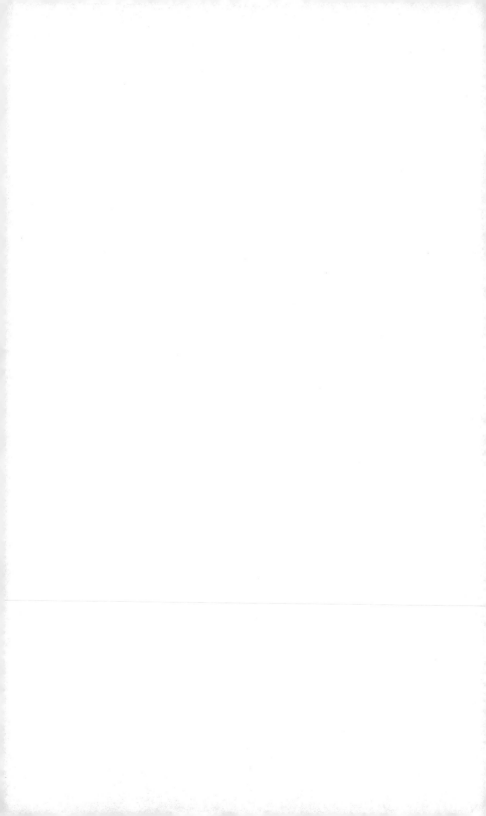

Explorers through the Mind of Idea Treasures

RICHARD FRANKLIN

abbott press®

A DIVISION OF WRITER'S DIGEST

Abbott Press books may be ordered through booksellers or by contacting:

Abbott Press
1663 Liberty Drive
Bloomington, IN 47403
www.abbottpress.com
Phone: 1-866-697-5310

ISBN: 978-1-4582-1522-2 (sc)
ISBN: 978-1-4582-1540-6 (hc)
ISBN: 978-1-4582-1523-9 (e)

Library of Congress Control Number: 2014906721

Printed in the United States of America.

Abbott Press rev. date: 04/21/2014

Contents

Grandma's Sunday Family

Dinner... 1

Laundry Pile.................................. 5

Night Castle 9

Ghost Friend 13

Crushed Ice................................. 17

Traveling through Cracks in a

Broken, Dead-End Road....... 21

Four Miles to Go 29

Dancing Animals 35

Coffee at Night............................41

Tree without Apple....................45

Ice-Skating in the Streets.........49

Shining above Cloudy Stars.....53

A Boxer without Punches

    Thrown....................................57

Magic inside the Water

    Bottles....................................65

Homeless, Giving Human........73

Spiritual Tendency....................77

Old Company...........................81

Creepy..............................89

Lost Footprints.....................97

Desire from the Far 105

Balling Like Nothing
    Happened.......................109

Dragon Dance.......................113

Onto the Court 119

Sunrise, My Sunset..................127

Her Smile, Her Style, My
    Everything......................131

Sharing the Wealth..................135

Dead in a Casket 143

Last Times 147

A Cutie in Slow-Motion

    Vision 153

Through the Dust 157

Dear Love 165

Gonna Make You Cry 175

About the Author 183

Grandma's Sunday Family Dinner

The table is set out for
everyone to sit down and eat,
Hugs and kisses on
Grandma for the food that
was made for the feast.
She sits down and looks at
the progress of what really

brings family together
while looking at the dinner
being eating all the way to
the heart of the belly—
A full smell of laughter and
overjoyed people coming from
the kitchen made Grandma's
dinner even better in harmony.

Laundry Pile

Everything could not
be situated and was
all left in a mess.
It crowded the place where
a person couldn't see
their reflection from the
morals inside of them.
The last chance to find peace
fell down in a pile, where

it was hard to find a true
meaning of truth to be seen
without anyone blocking it—
A pile where something was
referred to as unbelievable
because of how much weight
it held and the max a person
had to carry through a tunnel
of secrets, entering unwashed
problems that weren't solved.

Night Castle

A moon that froze far into
the night caught people
in a silent moment.
There was no time for a glass
of water when things started
freezing everywhere in sight.

The castle that was miles
away could be seen with a
light sitting above it even
though it was night.
Then out of nowhere, ice
began to melt from the
living sun in the castle
that made itself a home
through the dark spaces.

Ghost Friend

When no one is around,

he talks to himself

just to find self.

He found a friend out of

nowhere to prevent the hurt

from being all alone;

It was best that way, because

just he and his ghost friend

were all he needed to enjoy

and play to find a way.

Closed eyes under the
trees, listening to whispers
from a friend he can't see
because the only friend is
in him, glorying to be—
When no one is there, he
knows his ghost friend will
be standing close by to listen
with nothing but ears open.

Crushed Ice

Frozen to the core and sooner

or later going to melt by

how the heat is outdoors,

Ice came fast from the

freezer because of how many

bags were brought in.

Nothing but a crushing

sound was all a person

could hear as the ice would

be scooped up and put in

a cup, given to the people

who were worn out from

sweating all day from work,

the parents and kids who

played all day at the park—

A sensation given off by

the liquid ice to make

the body chilly and slide

through the veins as a

person elevated far from the

crushed ice that they felt.

Traveling through Cracks in a Broken, Dead-End Road

There's no space to even walk
or breathe; we have chosen to
lie down and receive failure or
stand up and believe that out
of all of us, we can succeed.
It is exposed to traveling
through cracks in a broken,
dead-end road to see how
far a person wants to go.

A man who gave his mind
and soul didn't ever let his ego
show because of the route he
been through and still has to
pass by in an orderly fashion.
With a loss of passion, he
still rises to the hype.

Bats flying down that dead-

end road with cracks exposed

in it to show photo pictures

of many who tried to conquer

their fear by tightening up

their gear and becoming

patient humans who don't care

about the circumstances of
traveling alone—because of
the feeling of them knowing
it will be home at the end of
the cracks, traveling through
the broken, dead-end road
with thin air to spare.

Four Miles to Go

Barbeque smoke coming from
the grill that's giving people
a run for their plates—
It has been a few days since
some people have eaten.
One plate to the kids
was all it took.

This was fueling people of different ages who needed to get prepared to run in the charity race, but that's when someone came through and cooked something delightful so they wouldn't be going on empty stomachs.

There couldn't be a better
day to come out to show
support for people who
needed it the most.
A toast to the ones who
took their marks and ran
like cheetahs in reach for a
prize position of healing.

Dancing Animals

A party filled with excitement
that included zebras, lions,
bears, tigers, monkeys, and
eagles eating cake in the
jungle of the noise of animals
that looked to keep the
fun going all night long,

Sparkles and fireworks were
part of the gathering of a
group that took over the dance
floor where the rest of their
crew who were considered
part of the team who
celebrated together as one—

Times could get tough from
here, but right then and there,
it was about getting to know
one another, not making a
meal or battle against someone
who looked like prey to the
eyes of the greedy teeth in
one's mouth that was meant
to sing songs and hold hands
while doing so at the dance.

Coffee at Night

Can't get that good night's
rest, seeing butterflies
flying over the bed,
Feels like lying outside just
without the stars but still
shows the dark and clouds
with the moon creating a smile
that takes a simple mind into a
space where there's no daytime
but there is no place to hide,

A smooth smell of the
keep-up to finish business to
further a mission: creating
a painting without using a
brush, just an imagination
that's timeless with a broken
watch that still can rekindle
a *tick-tock* from a taste of the
sip of coffee that keeps a
person on a steady go with a
rocket movement of motion.

Tree without Apple

Horses running out of there,
stable glass falling off the
shelves due to the storm,
Tears out of eyes that couldn't
close because it was so much
to witness inside the weary
night of sorrowing ghosts,
One place that was open
as a heart surgery was the
basement—behold apples
standing side by side,

Fruits started to later grow,

People then started

to later show,

Time of fault for the ones who

never were there to begin.

One look around—it was

vegetables on the tree that

lost plenty of sensation.

Ice-Skating in
the Streets

Cold breeze dragging along

teardrops written on the

downward eyes of a lost guy,

Matchmaking on skates

where people tried their

hardest not to fall and crack

a piece in the sensitive ice,

Underground shoveling where
dancing, free inmates were
trying to make their marks
on a cool night without the
faithful skates needed to
pass grabbing hands—
Senseless acts committed to
justify why there should be
better laws while ice-skating
down a dead-end hallway.

Shining above
Cloudy Stars

Spring has paved the way for
fall to the doorway with books
of thoughts and knowledge.
A free and open mind
moves at different points
in life—a happy grand
opening of similes—

One final dance that lasted in

the clouds, where stars relied

on a sparkling shine above

far, from being behind;

Flowers even grew in a pond

of watery clouds without shine

needed—only oxygen of lively

butterflies that represented

the shining clouds of stars

up above timeless gravity.

A Boxer without Punches Thrown

Words of encouragement to
leave people speechless—
There are no hard feelings
because he can see it through
the test of hard times.
Cracks in a broken mind,
Trying to find patients,
to not be left behind,

Looking to beat your
opponent just by using
your gift of freedom, of
bone-chilling words.
A person out doors of their
comfort, looking for a fight—
but the joke's become on them
because the only punches
thrown were confident of
being someone of a leader.

Teach the small-minded who
use the forces of weapons to
use the strength that harvests
a heart connected to the
mind of their own to show
him and her their destinies
have already been carved.

There isn't a need for a
battle or war zone to try to
conquer a point—the reason
punches weren't thrown
was because wisdom took
on the badge of honor.

Magic inside the Water Bottles

People watch the moon
turned across the galaxy,
splashing water into
magic of sand, floating
past bottles of crystals.
When will it be a day
someone sees they're only
giving days ahead?

No food or bread to nourish

the stomach of the sickening

people who didn't care if

it took walking through

broken glass for help.

Over a pathway where there
was a land of perished water
that shined, food that was
laid out for all to chow
on, and slices of bread to
make many meals for all,

Coming across something
that could never be held
inside people's minds for
years that would have been
some sort of magic in the
water bottles to keep them
around a little longer on
earth's golden, watered grass.

Homeless, Giving Human

Safe underneath the

rock of shields,

The only giving leftovers

were tears to spare;

People who made offerings

took care without any worries,

A show poured out for

the ones who meant the

most to the project.

Braved what was inherited
from the trash bags of
canned goods, clothes,
shoes, and other needy
material given from those
who never did have it,
Turned homeless but when
able to grasp any special
breath, it was worth every
single thing a person had just
to be held again into light.

Spiritual Tendency

With the blessings of
the angels showing each
one of us to death,
Make sure your heart is
running into his arm for
safety and protection so
people will love again.

We as people are accompanied
to share cultured living with
the belief of healing from
the Lord's ceiling of grace,
where it's an undefined place
with a matter of faith.

Old Company

Lost the mood to react to
a scale of misery, trying
to find company,
Wishing the one who brought
you joy a long time ago
could bring more instead
of taking it back with the
feeling of emptiness

It feels that you have to push forward and find new waves of attention to keep your interest at surfing. Cherish your puzzles that are full before someone tends to step on them and they begin to crumble.

Then the rebuild starts all
over again, just wishing for
a sign and a witness to be
among your glory of shade.

Another conversation of
people will come along and
spark up an old company
that you used to have
composite in your mind at
the center of the garden of
true lively from lonesome.

Creepy

A time of pleasant smells—
The flowers don't
grow or smell,
A clown tossing around
juggling balls,
Seventeen-foot man
standing tall,

Building sand castles

out of smashed clay,

Letting our minds

lead the way.

In my imagination, I

will always stay

Off the cliff to the sea,

Deeper into the ocean

on the shark back,

The last impression

without an act,

Smoking tobacco without

the site of smoke,

Invisible people playing

live music in their bands,

A horse singing songs

with a flute in his hand,

Your last memories

of the impossible

Stories come true.

Something so weird—

how could we let it be

In these crazy dreams that

have become reality?

Lost Footprints

An opening in the sand
that froze in the winter—
Missed communication
on what was there could
not be retraced
Past the tunnel of hope but
not the entering of daylight.

Support that was meant

for you but taken away

because the audience

thought otherwise of

the spiritual person

Cannot take them down,

because the footprints are

forever permanent, even

if they couldn't be seen.

This means the one
made by someone else
was lost but there.
Another person came
along and made some
impossible measurements.
They created deep footprints
of their own in the solid,
frozen ice of the sand.

The person created their
own path and destination
Until someone else came and
did the same; now theirs is
lost, but they already have
found their place in the
path of their own creation.

Desire from the Far

Skating on ice is so amazing
when I see you there—
How the ice flakes jump out
of the floor pavement every
time she lands a move.
One glance from the
corner of your eye will
take your breath away—

A star at night while she
skates on the magnificent
ice of sparkles.
It seems like I could sit down
and watch her skate for days.

Balling Like Nothing Happened

Watched the days wash
away your tears upon the
pride of a warrior,
They kept on fighting for
their last breath that might
guide them every day.

The money doesn't do anything but create a smile and frown because being stuck by needles fills the void, but time, past, and the present were almost closing the last piece of the sunset to awaken the sleepy who couldn't rise by themselves.

Dragon Dance

Dancing to the playful
time of drums of fire,
Looking across at the
one you admire,
Never passing up a chance
for a hug because there
are no good-byes going
to be mentioned—

Tension in the mind,
where the beat trembles for
attention of a two-step,
Out of the level without prep
but prepared to give the floor
a run for its pattern of people
who decided to compete.

Under a mask disguised in skin tends to address the attire placed with incredible skills of passion with bear claws of a driven mystery.

Onto the Court

After those jump shot

days are over,

The cold wind brings you

into an unshaped angle.

Trying as much as you

can to make things

comfortable for you,

The practice just

doesn't add up.

Count the free throws that

have been made at the basket;

Off-court decisions can
make something out of
nothing, but those free
throws have to be made.
Getting paid for bad decisions
can stair up the competition
Involved in all the
ball-handling scuffle
under the pile.

Leaving the court mad,
embarrassed, and badly
bruised—but the best
foot forward was taken
into concept—
Putting in more effort can
make a different outcome.
Entered with a prepared mind
but unprepared physically
for the battle ahead

While tracing memories
in the everyday buzzer
shots that were taken—
Do not be mistaken for those
purposeful opportunities
because time and will let you
see the brighter picture.
This gleaming storm of raise
could be the getaway jump
shot they were looking for.

Sunrise, My Sunset

Your body is amazing,
Your cold feet deep
like a razor.
Your bright mind is awesome
because you are rising.

A dose of you—now I'm flying behind the mountain creek to help you reach your peak of higher limits.

Her Smile, Her Style, My Everything

Give it back to me—

your heart you took from

the love of your life.

Let's take a trip—but

your body wants to be

still and never move

The way someone's eyes play
in tune with their soul.
My ambition lets me make her
smile and cry tears of silver,
A moment that will take you
here and there with a charm
on your wrist and arm.

Sharing the Wealth

It's all in a time and a place
to give and never waste—
The gift in the store for the
one who inherited a travel
guide to where the joy of
thoughtfulness comes from.

Pulling plums off a tree,

seeing a smile off the needy

because of how you shared

your own earned cash to make

the poor have a blast—

Something that their minds
and hearts will never forget,
and surely the place in your
storage of helping from the
beginning to show the right
duty of how the wealth shared
by never being over greedy

Without showing the people
how much they are valued
to you because things are
being done for what's best
inside so it can continue
to last forever in a time.

Dead in a Casket

Love the unloved for what
they don't have in life.
Pull a leaf off a tree for your
buried treasure of secrets that
lays in the eyes of pushing
the door for a day and
nighttime sigh of death—

A love for no one but your
soul. It does love forever, ever,
ever in the last overdose of
pills of removing the pain.

Last Times

There are moments enjoyed
or that just wandered
off in the sunset.
The sounds of trains and
cars shine from stars.
When you make your
move, you will know it;
only time will show it—

A smile with a grin.

Time is passing by with the

smooth touch of your chin,

So don't pack your bags; just

take yourself for the ride,

because where you going, it's

just going to be happiness

inside, so touch the gate and

wait for your time to shine,
because when you do, things
come through with this
movement of a life journey.
As you watch the time pass
by with the glisten of an eye,
What used to be is now in
the rearview of the sky.

A Cutie in
Slow-Motion Vision

To the girl he writes;

to the girl he wrote.

Her name was Cutie, the

one who sat at her desk and

made ways for a solution with

a sparkling smile that came

from a joke of laughter.

Doesn't Cutie wish to

take that journey?

Cutie ended up blossoming
into an amazing girl.
Then he stood behind
Cutie and opened doors
and pulled out her seat,
dressing as the gentleman
he was supposed to be.
To the girl he liked; to
the girl he wrote.

Through the Dust

Flying the planes toward

a cloudy road—

Where do we go from here?

Inside the cave of

everlasting love—

Can't see where to go with

all the fog in the way.

One footstep at a time,

like baby steps—

So much pressure to

keep going ahead.

Just stop right here

and take your pick.

From the moments that

cannot be recaptured

Under the trees lost in

the imaginations,

A splash of water onto

the floor pavement—

Only time can tell

everyday life

As we travel the islands

of wine glasses.

Maybe things could
last for the best—
Dusting ourselves off, getting
prepared for the next mission.

Dear Love

Only climbing to the

stairway of your heart—

A quest into your water

puddle of daylight,

The melted stones that

poured into your eyes.

So wonderful to stand

next to the deadline,

Putting yourself on

hold for another

With the cold body begging

for your warmth.

Good luck to the last heart

that challenged you,

Wondering if they were coming back to see if any of it was true. Let's take this moment to remember the love that pushed for open arms.

At last, we meet up to

discuss the next move

But hope it won't

leave a bruise.

The heart can only take so

much that can be prescribed.

"Eat your heart out," they say.

Rain, rain, go away; another
love will come again one day.
If it comes and I never wake,
With my heart you
can be sure to take.

Gonna Make You Cry

A picture in someone's eye

where the sight can't see,

The many accomplishments

that different parents got to

witness their children make—

Sometimes everything
wasn't so bright down the
way of bringing hope to
the eyes of families.
Dozens of flying teardrops
spreading down the face where
a smile took years to replace,

Sinking under moments
that should be happy and
full of nothing but Kodak
times when a parent can get
to a lovely place in a rocking
chair and let their hands
continue to press rewind.

The tearful chances that came to be were meant for certain people to cry out all the tears they had left in them to make room for a building they were going to see through every weather mountain view that stood.

About the Author

I was born in Memphis,
Tennessee.

I want to feel the void of
poetry with an impact of
bringing a perspective of
people in order to gain a image
of a portrait of many dreams
that crumble from pieces
that are shattered to become
whole again—thoughts that

bring peaceful frames of mind
into the lives of the creative
scenery of the reader and that
give me a legacy of capturing
driven passion that may
leave one's eyes breathless.

Always and Forever,
Sincerely,
Yours Truly,
Richie Rich Da Hearthrob

CPSIA information can be obtained at www.ICGtesting.com
Printed in the USA
LVOW11s0901100215

426442LV00001B/63/P